Vocal
Chamber
Music

Recent Researches in Music

A-R Editions publishes seven series of critical editions, spanning the history of Western music, American music, and oral traditions.

Recent Researches in the Music of the Middle Ages and Early Renaissance
Charles M. Atkinson, general editor

Recent Researches in the Music of the Renaissance
James Haar, general editor

Recent Researches in the Music of the Baroque Era
Christoph Wolff, general editor

Recent Researches in the Music of the Classical Era
Eugene K. Wolf, general editor

Recent Researches in the Music of the Nineteenth and Early Twentieth Centuries
Rufus Hallmark, general editor

Recent Researches in American Music
John M. Graziano, general editor

Recent Researches in the Oral Traditions of Music
Philip V. Bohlman, general editor

Each edition in *Recent Researches* is devoted to works by a single composer or to a single genre. The content is chosen for its high quality and historical importance, and each edition includes a substantial introduction and critical report. The music is engraved according to the highest standards of production using the proprietary software MusE, owned by Music│Notes.™

For information on establishing a standing order to any of our series, or for editorial guidelines on submitting proposals, please contact:

A-R Editions, Inc.
801 Deming Way
Madison, Wisconsin 53717

800 736-0070 (U.S. book orders)
608 836-9000 (phone)
608 831-8200 (fax)
http://www.areditions.com

RECENT RESEARCHES IN AMERICAN MUSIC, 35

John Knowles Paine

Vocal Chamber Music

Edited by John C. Schmidt

 A-R Editions, Inc.

Madison

A-R Editions, Inc., Madison, Wisconsin 53717
© 1999 by A-R Editions, Inc.

A-R Editions is pleased to support scholars and performers
in their use of *Recent Researches* material for study or performance. Subscribers to any of the *Recent Researches* series,
as well as patrons of subscribing institutions, are invited to
apply for information about our "Copyright Sharing
Policy."

Printed in the United States of America

ISBN 0-89579-447-0
ISSN 0147-0078

∞ The paper used in this publication meets the minimum
requirements of the American National Standard for
Information Sciences—Permanence of Paper for Printed
Library Materials, ANSI Z39.48-1984.

Contents

Introduction

Two immensely popular musical genres of the nineteenth century were the solo song and the partsong for unaccompanied voices. Both were intended for music making at home or in social gatherings, as well as in concert situations. John Knowles Paine, the premier American composer of the second half of the nineteenth century, has left us only a few examples of each genre.

The art song is a genre to which Paine was not deeply committed, for only eleven songs may be numbered among his compositions. Yet, of these, seven were published, and some achieved a notable degree of popularity. Four were published by Oliver Ditson in 1879 as op. 29—*Matin Song, I Wore your Roses Yesterday, Early Spring-time,* and *Mondnacht (Moonlight)*. Three later songs, from op. 40, were published by Arthur P. Schmidt in 1884–85—*A Bird upon a Rosy Bough, A Farewell,* and *Beneath the Starry Arch*. A fourth song from op. 40, *Music when Soft Voices Die,* was announced for publication, but I have found no trace of either a manuscript or a print. Three additional songs are found only in manuscript—*Spring, A Spring in the Desert I Found,* and *Clover Blossoms*. All of Paine's songs are well written for voice—expressive, lyrical, with interesting, effective accompaniments—and would afford a pleasant surprise to an audience of sensitive amateurs of the Lied, or art song.

Paine's four-part settings for unaccompanied male chorus all date from the Civil War period, 1863 to 1865, when he had just begun his tenure as Musical Instructor and Organist at Harvard University. Two were published during his lifetime. *Radway's Ready Relief,* a mock-serious, elaborate setting of an advertisement for a popular patent medicine, was first published privately by the Apollo Club, a Boston chorus, in 1883, and later by Oliver Ditson. *Soldier's Oath,* written for Harvard Commemoration Day in 1865, was published for the occasion. Of the four partsongs extant in manuscript, three are included in op. 14—*Funeral Hymn for a Soldier, The Summer Webs,* and *Minstrel's Song. Peace, Peace to Him That's Gone* does not have an opus number, but could well be part of op. 14. All are attractive, varied pieces, showing a definite skill in writing effectively for men's voices.

An additional work for male voices is the anthem *O Bless the Lord, My Soul*. It no doubt dates from the same period as the other partsongs, for Paine was actively involved with the Harvard chapel choir, for whom this was probably written. The manuscript has not survived, but it was published by the Boston Music Co. in 1911.

All of these works have been unavailable for many decades, and those extant only in manuscript have never been accessible to the general public. These works provide a welcome addition to the repertory, while providing additional insight into the early and middle career of this seminal composer.

The Composer

John Knowles Paine was born on 9 January 1839 in Portland, Maine, of solid Yankee stock; in fact, three of his ancestors had emigrated on the *Mayflower*. His father was a band leader, music publisher, and proprietor of a music store; his grandfather had built one of the first pipe organs in the state. Paine's early musical training was with Hermann Kotzschmar, a conservatory-trained musician from Dresden, who moved to Portland in 1849. Paine studied further with Haupt, Wieprecht, and others in Berlin from 1858 to 1861, where he attracted notice as an accomplished organist and composer. Returning to the United States, he soon moved to Boston and began a long association with Harvard University, first as Musical Instructor and Organist, eventually attaining a full professorship in 1875. He initiated the teaching of music courses for credit at Harvard, and established the first department of music in any American liberal arts college. His pupils—including composers John Alden Carpenter, Frederick S. Converse, Arthur Foote, Edward Burlingame Hill, Clayton Johns, and Daniel Gregory Mason, and writers Richard Aldrich, William F. Apthorp, Henry T. Finck, M. A. DeWolfe Howe, Henry Taylor Parker, and Owen Wister—virtually dominated the musical scene in the Northeast at the beginning of the twentieth century. Paine resigned from Harvard in 1905 and died on 25 April 1906.

Paine was among the first American composers to successfully pattern his works after mid-century European models, in particular those favored and taught in German and German-American circles. Although his training and orientation were decidedly conservative, Paine's musical style was anything but static: there is a steady development and broadening of compositional approach from the student works of the 1850s and early 1860s, through the mature, classically inspired works of the mid-1860s to late

1870s, to the more advanced, "chromatic-progressive" compositions from the late 1870s and after.[1]

American composers, from the middle decades of the nineteenth century onwards, faced a growing dichotomy between music for the popular taste and art music: music for entertainment vs. music of a higher purpose, music of a new seriousness;[2] Paine was the first to be involved with this conflict in ideals. Popular music of the time has been defined as music written for a single voice or a small group of singers, usually accompanied by a single chord-playing instrument, usually first performed and popularized in a secular stage entertainment, "composed and marketed with the goal of financial gain," and "designed to be performed by and listened to by persons of limited musical training and ability." Most popular songs began with a four- or eight-bar introduction, continued with a regularly-phrased verse in common melodic patterns, such as AABC, ABAC, AABA, or ABCB, followed by a refrain, usually for chorus, derived from part of the verse, and concluding with a short piano postlude; a predictable design easily grasped by an untrained public.[3] Art music, however, "had acquired a special status," and "one was *supposed* to think about it."

> This music, the argument went, had the capacity to do more than entertain; it inspired and elevated. Even though it might be instrumental and abstract, it spoke to the ethical side of humanity. Even though it might be secular, it was sacred, in an intangible way. It was moral, it was good, it was good for you. Such music was called art music.[4]

John Sullivan Dwight (1813–93), arbiter of musical taste in Boston for a generation, defined the differences between the two styles in an 1841 address before the Harvard Musical Association. He wished "to show the dignity of music, as an art, and to establish the power, so often claimed for it, of elevating the feelings and ennobling social life." He admitted that music used for amusement could "while away an idle hour, to refresh a weary mind, or extract the sting of sorrow." However, he felt that such music was indulgence. It "belongs to the ornamental, not the indispensable." It "cannot enrich, ennoble, purify and perfect the powers ands sensibilities of man." Michael Broyles summarizes Dwight's implications:

> whatever [in music] does not aspire to the pure and the abstract, and therefore does not enrich and ennoble, is not simply different; it is a corruption of the holy art itself. By definition it is not music and thus not worthy of consideration. It must not be tolerated, because it represents a threat to the very concept of music. Music that does not fit the canon can only be vulgar at best, with the implication that those who listen to such music are also. Little concession is made to the audience.[5]

Composers of the Second New England School chose not to be as strict with the divisions between art and entertainment as Dwight might have preferred. Arthur Foote, for example, preferred "the simple, directly communicative, comfortable to perform, and highly lyrical representation of song," striving to reach "close enough

to the preferences of the general public that [his songs] oftentimes won a popular following."[6] In Edward MacDowell's songs, "the melody is of fundamental consequence. . . . It shows a kinship to American folk song of Anglo-Celtic origin in its simplicity and somewhat formulaic traits. Above all, MacDowell tried to create a smooth, emotionally convincing, and rhythmically attractive tune to evoke the main expressive thrust of the poem."[7] Horatio Parker's songs, despite some elaborate piano parts, "were written to appeal to a wide public, and, without being sentimental, express post-Romantic fervor."[8] George W. Chadwick, however, took an early stand against writers of parlor songs, and "was determined to avoid in his songs the kind of commercial sound he grew to hate"; he denied himself "the common touch," and "seems to have cultivated the elegant tastes and gestures of his refined patrons." This is in contrast to his instrumental music, where "he was uninhibited in his invention of popular, whistleable, even vulgar tunes."[9]

Paine's vocal music shares the qualities of his fellow Second New England School composers. It is attractive melodically, with interesting piano accompaniments, unhackneyed form, and sensitive text setting. Although most works have definite popular appeal, they are far more sophisticated, more eloquent than the typical commercial parlor ballad. Paine strove instead to meet the standards of German Lieder composers, including Schubert, Loewe, Schumann, Franz, and Brahms. Robert Franz (1815–92) was a definite influence on Paine and his colleagues. Paine compared him with other composers:

> Loewe and Franz were specialists, but their songs are very unlike. In Germany, Loewe has been especially popular with the masses, while Franz, by his exquisite taste and feeling, appeals more strongly to cultivated musicians. In certain respects Franz and Schumann share with Schubert in the fulfilment of the highest ideal of the German Lied.[10]

Because of his affiliation with Harvard, Paine tended to remove himself from the popular tradition.

> His success in establishing music at Harvard inaugurated a trend that was to affect American musical composition into the late twentieth century: the association of the composer with academia. This freed the composer from the marketplace, allowing him and later her to write, for a limited and erudite audience, works that need not have a broad appeal or impact. It also constricted the composer. Endemic to the prime argument that secured music in academia, that it should be studied as literature, was the notion of a canon of great masterpieces worthy of such status. This placed a particular obligation on the academic composer, to write in that tradition. It provided a standard against which his work would be measured, and he knew it. It also fostered an innate conservatism, as the past as model and exemplar was always visible.[11]

Paine's experience with choral music began at an early age. As a teenager, prior to his studies in Berlin, he served as organist (1857–58) for Portland's choral society, the Haydn Association, and performed expert accompaniments for their performances of Handel's *Messiah*.[12] After his return from Berlin in 1861, he gave a concert at Portland's First Parish Church in which the church choir sang his *Agnus Dei* and *Benedictus* (both works written in 1861 and now lost).[13] He soon accepted a position as organist and choir director at Boston's historic West Church, which he held from 1861 to 1864.[14]

In March 1862, Paine joined the Harvard staff as "teacher of Sacred Music," teaching classes in vocal music, and later becoming director of music and organist, serving as daily organist, training the choir, and providing a substitute for Sunday morning services[15] because of his prior commitment to West Church. Paine's vocal music classes were very popular, and in September 1862 a group of law students petitioned the law faculty to organize a vocal class for themselves as well.[16] It is quite possible that several of Paine's settings for men's voices were composed for these groups, as well as for the college choir and the Harvard Musical Association.

Music and Texts

Paine's solo songs and works for small choral ensembles date from the middle part of his career. All of these works show his compositional craft, modeled in particular after the music of Beethoven, Mendelssohn, and Schumann. However, they also demonstrate his own individuality as a creative artist and the growth and development of his compositional style.

The earlier songs, as well as the partsongs, are from the period between the Mass in D (1865) and *St. Peter* (1870–72), and display a strong sense of tonality, sympathetic text setting, rhythmic variety, gracefully shaped phrases, occasional pentatonic melodic figures, and, in the songs, a variety of piano textures. Many stylistic features of these works are part of the common vocabulary of mid-nineteenth-century music, such as frequent pedal points, emphasis on plagal progressions, first-beat appoggiaturas or suspensions, mixed-mode chords (such as the subdominant and supertonic chord qualities borrowed from the parallel minor), and the melodic and harmonic use of the raised supertonic. Later songs demonstrate Paine's more "chromatic-progressive" style of the Second Symphony (1879) and the music to *Oedipus Tyrannus* (1880–81), with increasing use of mediant key relationships, enharmonic chord use, including the "omnibus" progression,[17] altered dominants, and linear non-functional chord relationships.

In addition, Paine was eclectic in his choice of poems. A number of them were by Boston-area authors, either acquaintances or close friends, several associated with Boston's *Atlantic Monthly*, while others were from popular eighteenth- and nineteenth-century lyricists, such as Josef Freiherr von Eichendorff, Thomas Chatterton, and Thomas Moore.

Songs

Matin Song

The first of Paine's songs to be published was *Matin Song*, the first in a series of monthly musical supplements to *Atlantic Monthly* for 1877:

contributions of original music by such composers as J. K. Paine, George L. Osgood, Dudley Buck and Francis Boott, with words by some of the most distinguished *Atlantic* poets.[18]

Atlantic editor William Dean Howells commissioned and published five songs (of a projected twelve) as a means of boosting lagging circulation. Publishing songs in a literary monthly was an unusual step, serving to promote popular art-song style of composers such as Robert Franz—preferred by the "gentle" tradition—over such common commercial hits of the day as *I'll Take You Home Again, Kathleen* and *In the Gloaming*.[19]

Matin Song was the most popular and widely published of Paine's songs, and shows the composer at his best. Bayard Taylor's poem is set gracefully, with notable sensitivity and rhythmic variety, and with "great interest and spontaneity," as William Treat Upton described the song.[20] Paine's strophic setting is straightforward, with a melodic charm that could satisfy the tastes of the wider public. However, other features of Paine's style demanded greater sophistication of the performer and listener, including freely resolved appoggiaturas and suspensions (mm. 3 and 12), pedal point, plagal progressions, the melodic turn (m. 9), mixed mode chords (mm. 3 and 5), and altered dominants (see the augmented dominant seventh chord and its irregular resolution in mm. 10–11). Dominant minor ninths and thirteenths add color to the cadence in the piano postlude, and raised fourths provide a chromatic preparation for the fifth degree.

Clara Doria premiered *Matin Song* on 17 January 1877 at Harvard's Sanders Theatre, only shortly after it was published in the January 1877 issue of *Atlantic Monthly*. Nine other performances have been documented, by artists such as Fanny Kellogg, Mrs. Otis Rockwood, Lillian Stoddard, Mrs. Anne Kennard-Martin, Paul Savage, and Harrison Bennett.[21]

Poet Bayard Taylor (1825–78) first achieved success as an author with *Views Afoot* (1846), which detailed a two-year walking tour of Europe. A long career as a travel journalist ensued, including reports for Horace Greeley's New York *Tribune* on the California gold rush, the Middle East, and Commodore Perry's expedition to Japan. Despite these many successes and his great demand as a lecturer, Taylor longed for recognition as a serious poet—but critic R. H. Stoddard termed him a verse-maker, not a poet. His best work is found in *Home Pastorals* (1875), as well as his excellent metrical translation of Goethe's *Faust*.[22]

I Wore your Roses Yesterday

Varied piano textures enhance Paine's setting of Celia Thaxter's *I Wore your Roses Yesterday*, which Upton pronounced "delightfully lyric and graceful."[23] Harmonic elements include a rather complex setting for "defying all the storms of fate" (mm. 34–38), employing part of the omnibus progression, as well as the close of the first verse in C major (mm. 9–11), the major mediant key, and the delicate setting of "ev'ry thought of you a rose" (mm. 49–51), emphasizing the supertonic. Other chromatic forays include augmented dominant sevenths and a diminished seventh on the raised submediant. Paine was sparing in his use of non-harmonic tones in the melody, save for an appoggiatura at the final cadence of each verse and a pedal point in the haunting piano postlude. One of Paine's former students, tenor George L. Osgood, performed *I Wore your Roses Yesterday* on a 7 February 1881 concert featuring Polish violinist Timotheus Adamowski;[24] the *Boston Daily Advertiser* reviewer called Paine's song "an expressive lay, though the theme is of a wandering sort."[25]

Celia Laighton Thaxter (1835–94) was the daughter of Thomas Laighton, a successful Portsmouth, N. H., merchant, editor, and legislator, who, disappointed in his quest for the governorship, exiled himself and his family to the remote Isles of Shoals, off the Maine–New Hampshire coast, in 1839. The family opened a summer hotel, Appledore House, in 1848, which became an artist colony, attracting such figures as authors James Russell Lowell, John Greenleaf Whittier, Henry M. Alden, Sarah Orne Jewett, and James and Annie Fields, artists J. Appleton Brown, William M. Hunt, Ross Turner, and Childe Hassam, and musicians Paine, William Mason, Julius Eichberg, and Arthur Whiting. Thaxter was a poet-naturalist; her supreme passion was a love of flowers. Many of her poems were published in *Atlantic Monthly*, including *I Wore your Roses Yesterday* (August, 1875), and her very popular sketchbook, *Among the Isles of Shoals* (1873), which went through seventeen editions in twenty years, was first serialized in the *Atlantic*.[26] Thaxter was a special friend of the Paines, and visited their home in Cambridge during the winter of 1880–81 when Paine was composing his music for Sophocles' *Oedipus Tyrannus*.[27]

EARLY SPRING-TIME

Rupert Hughes called *Early Spring-time* "most curiously original," and Henry T. Finck felt that it has "a peaceful, almost religious character, suggesting the composer's sacred works."[28] Thomas Hill's free verse is set as a quasi-recitative, with cross accents that purposely weaken the effect of the meter. The tonality is ambiguous as well, shifting between C-sharp minor and E major, with a remarkable final half-cadence in the piano postlude. (This ending was a later addition; there is no postlude in the earlier version preserved in the autograph manuscript.) The absence of a raised leading tone at the beginning gives a modal effect (mm. 5–11), and the harmonic setting of "Death is but frost" is startling (mm. 28–30). Paine's manuscript is dated 28 June 1866, placing its composition during the time when Hill was president of Harvard.

Thomas Hill (1818–91) was a Unitarian clergyman, who, beginning in 1845, following his seminary training at Harvard, served for fourteen years as a minister at Waltham, Massachusetts. During 1859 to 1862 he was president of Antioch College in Ohio. He then served as president of Harvard from 1862 to 1869. In 1873 he began eighteen years' service at First Parish Church in Portland, Maine. Along with published treatises on arithmetic and geometry, he wrote numerous poems, many religious in nature; a collection was published as *In the Woods and Elsewhere* in 1888.[29] He was the grandfather of the composer Edward Burlingame Hill (1872–1960), one of Paine's most successful students.

MONDNACHT

Paine set each of the two sections of the German poet Josef Freiherr von Eichendorff's popular *Mondnacht* to different music. In the second part, Paine uses techniques of linear, non-functional chord progressions to avoid internal cadences, thus constantly increasing tension to an eventual broad climax. Paine's setting is well matched to the original German poem, and the manuscript was planned for the German text, although an incomplete "singing English" version was added above the vocal staff. In the published version a complete English text was included, although it differs some from the manuscript alignment and its text repetitions do not fit the music as naturally as those in the German setting. The manuscript is dated 1867, from about the time of the successful performance of Paine's Mass in Berlin.

Eichendorff was a major figure of German literary Romanticism and an important source of musical Romanticism in the nineteenth century. His poems were set hundreds of times as solo songs with piano accompaniment, as partsongs, as cantatas, and in other genres; according to one study, there were over five thousand settings of Eichendorff texts in the nineteenth century. Eichendorff poems were attractive to the composer because of their folk-like quality, often modeled after the folk poetry of Achim von Arnim and Clemens Brentano's folk anthology *Des Knaben Wunderhorn* (1806–08). Strophic structure, straightforward rhyme schemes, simplicity of diction, and effective use of poetic landscapes attracted many composers to Eichendorff's poetry.[30]

SPRING

Vivid contrasts in piano textures are seen in *Spring*, an unpublished song dated "August 9, 1869, Constableville, N. Y.," less than a month before Paine's marriage. Simple, repeated eighth-note chords at the beginning are replaced by almost orchestral figurations in the central portion; in addition, occasional rhythmic freedom in the vocal line suggests operatic recitative (m. 8) and cadenza (m. 17). Particularly effective are the bass "gloom" motive (mm. 9–12), the depiction of the winter storms (mm. 12–24), and the "flee away" retransition to the beginning material (mm. 14–16). The poem has no attribution in the manuscript.

A SPRING IN THE DESERT I FOUND

Another unpublished song is *The Fountain*, or *A Spring in the Desert I Found*, written about 1878. There is a gothic agony in George Parsons Lathrop's poem that is captured admirably in Paine's music. It is Paine's only song in a minor key throughout; this mode combines with the restlessness of the piano figuration to enhance the stark drama of the text. The strophic plan is modified in the second verse by higher melodic peaks and phrase extensions at the midpoint (mm. 32–39) and the ending (mm. 49–55), contributing to the growth and climax of the song. Balanced phrases combine to form broad melodic arches, whose controlled tension attests to Paine's superb craftsmanship.

George Parsons Lathrop (1851–98) devoted his life to writing a series of novels, short stories, history, and poems. After studying law at Columbia Law School, he joined the editorial staff of *Atlantic Monthly* (1875–77) and the Boston *Sunday Courier* (1877–79). Many of his poems appeared in magazines and periodicals. An important volume of his poems was *Rose and Roof-Tree* (1875). His poetry was judged by a contemporary to be "rushing and vigorous, though not deficient in that subtle work which leaves the reader at the boundary of some elevating thought." Lathrop married Rose Hawthorne, daughter of Nathaniel Hawthorne, in 1871. He edited Hawthorne's works for publication,[31] and prepared the libretto for Walter Damrosch's opera, *The Scarlet Letter*, which was produced successfully in Boston in the 1895–96 season.[32] The Lathrops were friends of Paine—Henry T. Finck recalls meeting Rose Hawthorne at the Paines' residence.[33]

CLOVER BLOSSOMS

Oscar Laighton's simple poem, *Clover Blossoms*, was set sympathetically and effectively by Paine; his manuscript, dated 1 October 1882, was never published. Warm piano textures enrich the poem's emotion, particularly where octave doublings of the melody produce almost orchestral sonorities (see mm. 7–8 and 14). Frequent non-harmonic tones (appoggiaturas, suspensions, and accented passing tones) give momentum to the vocal line, beginning with its first pitch. Surprising elements include the harmonic twist in mm. 54–57 and the novel ending, which teases us into expecting more, then relents and concludes.

Oscar Laighton (1839–1939), brother to Celia Thaxter, was one of the managers of Appledore House, Isles of Shoals. His *Clover Blossoms* was the result of one of his many summer romances:

> Our island was a paradise for young lovers. There was delight and romance in the very air, in the sparkle of the water and magic of the star-lit nights. Hardly a summer passed without an engagement, and one season there were five. I earnestly endeavored to bring the number up to six, but could not seem to make the young lady I was so fond of that year understand the importance of this. She was ever sweet to me, but elusive. We were often sailing together in my whaleboat, which she learned to manage as I lay at her feet. One day the beloved and I were walking through the field of red clover in front of the hotel, leading up to my sister's cottage garden fence. In sister's parlor William Mason was playing delightfully. That was fifty years ago, yet I recall the lovely day and delicious murmur of the water about the coves. That evening I wrote a song to my sweetheart, venturing to show it to Mr. Whittier, who, with his sister, Elizabeth, was staying at Appledore that summer. Mr. Whittier seemed pleased with my verse, saying, "Thee did well, Oscar." He

sent it to the *Atlantic Monthly,* and, to my astonishment, it was published in that conservative magazine.[34]

A BIRD UPON A ROSY BOUGH

The ongoing restlessness and chromaticism of *A Bird upon a Rosy Bough* enhances the bittersweet urgency of Celia Thaxter's poem. The rushing accompaniment attracted Upton, who commented on the "rich and sonorous piano score."[35] Phrase structure is regular, and there are few non-harmonic tones in the melodic line until the conclusion, when in the last seven bars appoggiaturas, suspensions, dominant thirteenths, and the melodic turn—all Paine devices—are used to enhance the closing text.

A FAREWELL

A Farewell is a simple strophic setting of Charles Kingsley's poem. Much of the melody is basically pentatonic, and each phrase ends with an appoggiatura or a suspension. Final cadences incorporate a dominant thirteenth. It was performed by George J. Parker on an Arthur Foote concert in Chickering Hall, Boston, on 15 March 1887;[36] a writer for the *Post* found *A Farewell* to be "among the best" of the songs, and the *Advertiser's* reviewer remarked, "Professor Paine's [song] was of a good commonplace style."[37]

Charles Kingsley (1819–75) was an English clergyman highly involved in the social reform movements of his time. His earliest novels, *Alton Locke* and *Yeast,* deal with Christian Socialism, and his best-known works are the historical romances *Hypatia, Westward Ho!,* and *Hereward the Wake,* and his fairy tale *The Water Babies.*[38] His poem, *A Farewell,* was written for his niece in February 1856.[39]

BEYOND THE STARRY ARCH

Harriet Martineau's poem *Beyond the Starry Arch* shows a mood of real determination, and Paine's music fits it well. Regular phrases are found except at the end, where text repetition and chromatic progressions delay the final cadence. Frequent non-harmonic tones include a chordal appoggiatura (m. 5), accented passing tones and appoggiaturas (see mm. 6, 8, 9), and a final pedal point. In measure 14, staccato chords punctuate "Hark to the foot fall"—an interruption of the prevailing accompaniment demanded by the text.

Harriet Martineau (1802–76), an English author, wrote extensively on religion, economics, and government. Her feelings against slavery were intensified by a trip to the United States in 1834–35, and she published her unfavorable critiques in *Society in America* (1837) and *A Retrospect of Western Travel* (1838). Among her most popular works were a series of children's stories, *The Playfellow* (1841).[40]

Partsongs

Paine wrote his partsongs for men's voices during the height of the Civil War, and most show an understandable preoccupation with death. All show Paine's clear understanding of the specific requirements of writing for male chorus. Chord voicings, practical tessituras, natural voice leading, variety of textures, and sensitive text settings are indications of his style and expertise. Paine's settings range from simple homophony to intricate partwriting of an almost virtuosic level.

Funeral Hymn for a Soldier

Funeral Hymn for a Soldier is a straightforward, hymn-like dirge that shows Paine's skill in working with sonorities for men's voices, whose close harmonies required a different style from SATB church harmony. Dotted rhythms and fanfare-like figures suggest a military cortège. Careful dynamic indications enhance the text. Octave doublings emphasize the words "Glory and grief." The poet was not acknowledged in the manuscript. It may have been a friend or colleague, perhaps even Paine himself.

The Summer Webs

The Summer Webs must have been intended to provide relief from the seriousness of the war. Its rhythmic style, antiphonal effects, and occasional humorous touches provide a welcome contrast to the *Funeral Hymn*. But the seriousness of the times is shown in the chromaticism and sudden pianissimo of "with naught to wake one sigh, except the wish that all we love were at this moment nigh." Again, the author of the text is not identified in the manuscript. The poem seems to be from an earlier period.

Minstrel's Song

A musically archaic style characterizes *Minstrel's Song*, in keeping with its eighteenth-century text. Harmonies are more diatonic, and there are some imitative effects. But Paine still includes a portion of the omnibus progression at "cold he lies in the grave below" (mm. 42–49), and mention of the raven and the death owl elicits prominent diminished-seventh chords (mm. 76–77 and 84–85).

Minstrel's Song sets the first five verses of a song from *Ælla, a tragycal enterlude, or discoorseynge tragedie,* the masterpiece of poet Thomas Chatterton (1752–70), written under the pseudonym Thomas Rowley. While a schoolboy at the church of St. Mary Redcliffe, Bristol, Chatterton found scraps of ancient parchment and used them to fabricate poems by an imaginary fifteenth-century monk, Thomas Rowley, supposedly attached as a secular priest to St. John's Church, Bristol. Chatterton presented a copy of *Ælla* to a bookseller in 1768, with hopes of obtaining publication. He began to acknowledge his authorship about this time, but this fact was not widely known, nor were his works published until after he took his life in August 1770.[41] Chatterton's brief, tragic life and remarkable work made him a hero to Romantic and Pre-Raphaelite poets. Wordsworth called him "the marvellous Boy," and Keats and Coleridge wrote poems about him.[42]

Peace, Peace to Him That's Gone

Paine's setting of Thomas Moore's *Peace, Peace to Him That's Gone* frames the text with a very placid homophonic texture, notwithstanding sharply dissonant appoggiaturas in measures 2 and 10 and a cadence in the key of the major mediant (G-sharp) at the end of the first phrase. Subsequent passages vary the texture significantly, and Paine is very careful in his placement of dynamic indications. There are two settings of the text beginning "Yet, oh, were mine one sigh of thine"; both are included in this edition. The second version is less demanding to perform, owing to its reliance on octave doublings, but both versions stress chromatic mediant key relationships, C major in the original, and G major in Version 2.

Peace, Peace to Him That's Gone is a setting of one of the Irish Melodies of the popular Irish poet, Thomas Moore (1779–1852). His *Irish Melodies,* with music by Sir John Stevenson, were issued in ten numbers between 1807 and 1834. Their popularity established him as the national poet of Ireland.[43]

Radway's Ready Relief

Radway's Ready Relief is a mock pretentious setting, in the style of a cantata, for a patent medicine whose advertisements saturated the newspapers of the early 1860s. Paine explained the circumstances:

> *Radway's Ready Relief* was composed in 1864, a youthful jest on my part, suggested by an advertisement I saw in the newspaper, and written for some friends of mine in Portland, Me.—my birthplace.[44]

This composition is full of musical humor, including the animated setting of "Esquire," the use of "Cuba" to form nonsense syllables in instrumental style, staccato bass notes in the doloroso section, also instrumental in style, and a solo bass recitative recalling the best oratorio style. The greatest humor is in the conclusion, which includes a quotation of the closing of Beethoven's *Egmont* Overture, with the tenors singing a patter song figuration with the repeated words, "ev'rywhere for sale by all apothecaries in the land, including Chelsea Beach." There is even Beethoven's piccolo part at the end ("to be whistled" per the instructions in the original). The Apollo Club of Boston performed *Radway's Ready Relief* on 25 April 1883 and repeated it the next year. Other performances were reported by organizations in Cincinnati, Albany, and New York, and Paine's friend John Fiske recalled an informal rendition at the Shoals.

> Monday went to Appledore, Isles of Shoals, taking Abby and Maud. . . . It was devilish hot in Boston, cool at Appledore. Had a deluge of music all through the visit. Monday evening orgy of Beethoven and Chopin by Paine, and beautiful songs by Clara Doria Rogers. . . . Tuesday morning . . . ramble on the rocks with the Paines. . . . Wednesday went to the Pavilion with Abby. In afternoon songs in big hall with Maud's accompaniment, also songs by Maud. . . . In evening had fine audience to hear "Las Casas," also given in big hall. From there to Celia's parlour for another hour of music. Miss Diana and Miss Benedict accompanists. And we had "Radway's Ready Relief" by Paine, which brought forth peals of laughter.[45]

However, not all listeners recognized the humor in *Radway's Ready Relief*. Following a performance by New York's Mendelssohn Glee Club, reviewer "H. H." complained:

It is ... a matter of regret, and was evidently so regarded by some of the truest friends of the [Mendelssohn] club, that it should have blotted one of its fair programmes with the words of Mr. J. K. Paine's song, with which the concert was concluded, and have given its attention to such trash. The title of this delectable composition is "Radway's Ready Relief," and the words set forth *in extenso* the value of that compound. Since the position of the Mendelssohn Glee Club makes it impossible to believe that its programmes would be used for the purpose of advertising a patent medicine, one is forced to the conclusion that the words of this song are intended to be facetious. As a matter of fact it would be difficult to imagine anything more haft [*sic*] witted and silly. Their perusal is calculated to produce an emotion of profound melancholy. If "Radway's Ready Relief" possesses the medical value which Mr. J. K. Paine claims for it, it would be a good thing for him to saturate himself freely with it before he writes another song. But for the Mendelssohn Glee Club the kindest advice is to avoid "Radway's Ready Relief," and thereby get rid of pain.[46]

The product, Radway's Ready Relief, manufactured by Radway & Co., New York, admittedly contained twenty-seven percent alcohol, and was advertised to relieve "rheumatism, sore throat, pleurisy, pneumonia, headache, burns and scalds, spinal affections, fevers, dysentery, cholera, paralysis," as a "preventive against the formation of concretions, gravel, or calculi," and as a "cure for Rheumatic and Malarious Complaints." Government controls ultimately tightened in the early twentieth century, and when the Bureau of Chemistry analyzed the preparation it found that it was essentially "a watery alcoholic solution of oleoresin of capsicum (cayenne pepper), camphor, and ammonia." Government officials ruled that the product was misbranded, that the statements regarding the curative effects were "false and fraudulent" and were applied "in disregard of their truth or falsity."[47]

SOLDIER'S OATH

Soldier's Oath was written for Commemoration Day at Harvard in 1865, held on the Friday of Commencement week to honor the 528 Harvard sons who had fought for the Union in the Civil War and to revere the memory of the ninety-three who had died. It shows the skill that the twenty-six-year-old musician had developed in producing interest and variety within a very limited format. For example, at the end of the first phrase is a half cadence in the relative minor, D minor. This does not provide the degree of punctuation that a cadence in the expected tonic key would, and consequently the music flows without break, as does the poetry. Additional contrasts are provided by the unison octaves in measures 5–6 and rhythmic imitation and sequence in measures 9–11. John Sullivan Dwight found *Soldier's Oath* to be "a spirited part-song."[48]

The poet of *Soldier's Oath*, Charles Timothy Brooks (1813–83), was a Unitarian clergyman and a graduate of Harvard College and Harvard Divinity School. He served as pastor to a church in Newport, Rhode Island, from 1837 to 1871, and was also known as a poet and a translator, especially from German (Schiller, Goethe, and Rückert).[49]

O BLESS THE LORD, MY SOUL

O Bless the Lord, My Soul is a straightforward tripartite setting of an Isaac Watts hymn text, probably composed for the Harvard chapel choir. Paine varied the texture through pairing, solo voices, and unison and octave passages. The organ part is supportive in the main, except for two short interludes. Contrasts in key are found in the middle portion, with references to A minor, C, and F.

Isaac Watts (1674–1748), the famous Calvinist clergyman, had a profound effect on the development of British and American Protestant church music; many of his several hundred hymn texts are widely used to this day. *O Bless the Lord, My Soul*, a versification of Psalm 103, first appeared in Watts' *The Psalms of David* (1719).[50]

Notes

1. For additional biographical information, see John C. Schmidt, *The Life and Works of John Knowles Paine* (Ann Arbor: UMI Research Press, 1980); and *The New Grove Dictionary of American Music*, s.v. "Paine, John Knowles," by Kenneth C. Roberts, Jr.

2. Michael Broyles, "Art Music from 1860 to 1920," in *The Cambridge History of American Music*, ed. David Nicholls (Cambridge: Cambridge University Press, 1998).

3. Charles Hamm, *Yesterdays: Popular Song in America* (New York: W. W. Norton, 1979), xvii, 254–55.

4. Broyles, "Art Music," 214–15.

5. Michael Broyles, *"Music of the Highest Class": Elitism and Populism in Antebellum Boston* (New Haven: Yale University Press, 1992), 257; the above statements from Dwight, "Address, Delivered before the Harvard Musical Association, August 25, 1841," are quoted by Broyles.

6. Nicholas E. Tawa, *Arthur Foote: A Musician in the Frame of Time and Place* (Lanham, Maryland: The Scarecrow Press, 1997), 143–44.

7. Nicholas E. Tawa, *The Coming of Age of American Art Music: New England's Classical Romanticists* (New York: Greenwood Press, 1991), 134.

8. William K. Kearns, *Horatio Parker, 1863–1919: His Life, Music, and Ideas* (Metuchen, N. J.: The Scarecrow Press, 1990), 184.

9. Victor Fell Yellin, *Chadwick, Yankee Composer* (Washington, D.C.: Smithsonian Institution Press, 1990), 158–59.

10. John Knowles Paine and Leo R. Lewis, "Music in Germany," in *Famous Composers and their Works*, ed. John Knowles Paine, Theodore Thomas, and Karl Klauser (Boston, 1891).

11. Broyles, "Art Music," 238–39.

12. Records, Haydn Association, 44, Portland, Maine, Public Library (MeP), and *Eastern Argus* (Portland, Me.) (28 December 1857): 2.

13. *Boston Musical Times* 2:13 (5 October 1861): 198.

14. Records of the Committee of the West Boston Society Corporation I (1806–64), 253, Boston Public Library (MB); *Dwight's Journal of Music* 24:2 (16 April 1864): 223.

15. Letters from A. P. Peabody to Hon. John A. Lowell, 18 and 25 March 1862, Letters of Acting President Andrew P. Peabody, 16 and 22, Harvard University archives (MH-Ar).

16. Harvard College Papers, Second Series, 29:328, Harvard University archives (MH-Ar).

17. According to Victor Fell Yellin, *The Omnibus Idea* (Warren, Michigan: Harmonie Park Press, 1998), 3, "the omnibus progression may be described as a chain of five chords beginning with (1), a dominant seventh in the first inversion, the root in the soprano. While the inner voices, tenor and alto forming the interval of the minor third, remain stable as pedals or double pedal, the two outer voices, soprano and bass, expand by contrary motion in four chromatic steps. The resulting chords, (2), (3), (4), and (5) are not as easily named. But the central chord (3) can be recognized as a minor six-four chord bracketed by chords (2) and (4), each taken as either a dominant seventh or augmented sixth. The series ends with chord (5), the same harmony as chord (1), but in root position, the third in the soprano."

18. *Boston Daily Advertiser* (9 October 1876): 4. Poets included Taylor, Celia Thaxter, Edmund C. Stedman, W. W. Story, and George Parsons Lathrop; composers also included Julius Eichberg. Five songs were published, the last appearing in the October 1877 issue.

19. Joseph A. Mussulman, *Music in the Cultured Tradition: A Social History of Music in America, 1870–1900* (Evanston: Northwestern University Press, 1971), 176–77.

20. William Treat Upton, *Art-Song in America* (Boston: Oliver Ditson, 1930), 78.

21. Many performances of songs went unrecorded, for voice recitals often did not receive detailed coverage in the press. Performance details of *Matin Song* and other Paine songs were gathered from newspaper reviews in the *Boston Daily Advertiser*, concert reports in *Dwight's Journal of Music, Musical Courier*, and program leaflets and clippings contained in Arthur Foote, comp., Three Scrap-Books of Clippings, Programs, etc., relating to music, Boston Public Library (MB).

22. *The National Cyclopaedia of American Biography* (hereafter cited as *NCAB*) vol. 3 (1893), s.v. "Taylor, Bayard"; and Willard Thorp, "Defenders of Ideality," in *Literary History of the United States*, 3d ed., ed. Robert E. Spiller, et al. (New York: Macmillan Co., 1963), 819, 821-23.

23. Upton, *Art-Song*, 78.

24. *Dwight's Journal of Music* 41:7 (26 March 1881): 53.

25. *Boston Daily Advertiser* (8 February 1881): 1.

26. *NCAB*, vol. 1 (1891), s.v. "Thaxter, Celia (Laighton)"; and Carlos Baker, "Delineation of Life and Character," in *Literary History of the United States*, 847.

27. Annie Fields, *Authors and Friends* (Boston: Houghton, Mifflin & Co., 1893), 247.

28. Rupert Hughes and Arthur Elson, *American Composers*, rev. ed. (Boston: The Page Co., 1914), 163; Henry T. Finck, *Songs and Song Writers* (New York: Charles Scribner's Sons, 1913), 232.

29. *NCAB*, vol. 6 (1896), s.v. "Hill, Thomas."

30. *One Hundred Years of Eichendorff Songs*, ed. Jurgen Thym, Recent Researches in the Music of the Nineteenth and Early Twentieth Centuries, 5 (Madison: A-R Editions, 1983).

31. *NCAB*, vol. 9 (1907), s.v. "Lathrop, George Parsons."

32. Walter Damrosch, *My Musical Life* (New York: Charles Scribner's Sons, 1923), 114–15.

33. Henry T. Finck, *My Adventures in the Golden Age of Music* (New York: Funk and Wagnalls, 1926), 77.

34. Oscar Laighton, *Ninety Years at the Isles of Shoals* (Boston: Beacon Press, 1930), 75–76.

35. Upton, *Art-Song*, 78.

36. Foote, Three Scrapbooks, vol. 1; the following *Post* clipping is also from this source.

37. *Boston Daily Advertiser* (16 March 1887): 4.

38. *The Reader's Encyclopedia*, 2nd ed., ed. William Rose Benét (New York: Thomas Y. Crowell, 1965), s.v. "Kingsley, Rev. Charles."

39. *Charles Kingsley: His Letters and Memories of his Life* (London: Macmillan & Co., 1901), 2:236.

40. *The Dictionary of National Biography* (hereafter cited as *DNB*) (1917), s.v. "Martineau, Harriet."

41. *DNB*, s.v. "Chatterton, Thomas"; *Ælla* is found in *The Poetical Works of Thomas Chatterton* (London: G. Bell & Sons, Ltd., 1915), vol. 2.

42. *The Oxford Companion to English Literature*, 5th ed., ed. Margaret Drabble (Oxford: Oxford University Press, 1985), s.v. "Chatterton, Thomas."

43. *DNB*, s.v. "Moore, Thomas."

44. *Musical Record* 267 (April 1884): 2.

45. 25 August 1890 letter in Ethel F. Fisk, ed., *The Letters of John Fiske* (New York: Macmillan, 1940), 581.

46. From an unidentified, undated clipping glued into a copy of the score; Boston Public Library (MB).

47. Arthur J. Cramp, *Nostrums and Quackery* (Chicago: American Medical Association, 1921), 2:738.

48. *Dwight's Journal of Music* 25:10 (5 August 1865): 79.

49. *Dictionary of American Biography* (1929), s.v. "Brooks, Charles Timothy."

50. *A Dictionary of Hymnology*, 2nd ed., ed. John Julian (1907; reprint, New York: Dover, 1957), s.v. "Watts, Isaac."

Songs

Matin Song

Op. 29, No. 1

Bayard Taylor

I let the dear - est dream de - part That night to love re-vealed, Some ea-ger spir-it in my heart___ My sleep - ing eyes un - sealed. Yet still 'twas love that led me here And bids my feet de - lay. A - rise, and light the dawn, my dear! Look___ forth, look forth and bring___ the day.

As out of dark - ness yon-der star Of whit - est ray is

born, As birds and blos-soms feel a - far ____ The com - ing of the morn, So thou hast dawn'd, and

now art near, To bright - en and to stay: My be - ing dies in thine, my dear! As ____

____ day - break dies _____ in day.

I Wore your Roses Yesterday

Op. 29, No. 2

Celia Thaxter

warm wind sweeps These ai - ry folds like va - por ___ fine, ___

A - mong them still the o - dor sleeps, And

haunts me with a dream di - vine, a dream di - vine.

And ev' - ry thought _____ of you, ev' - ry thought of you a

rose!

Early Spring-time

(Frühzeitiger Lenz)
Op. 29, No. 3

Thomas Hill

None can ex - press the ___ long - ing, the long - ing
Wer mal - te wohl das ___ Seh - nen, das Seh - nen so

min - gled with ___ joy, min - gled with sad - ness, swell - ing my
rauh an sel' - ger Lust, rauh auch an Thrä - nen, das stets durch

heart ___ e - ver, When A - pril brings us the bird and ___ flower.
mei - ne See - le klingt, wenn Lenz uns Vö - gel und Blüm - lein ___ bringt.

Mondnacht

(Moonlight)
Op. 29, No. 4

Josef Freiherr von Eichendorff

Andante con moto

Es war, als hätt' der Him - mel Die
It seemed that earth while sleep - ing, Re -

Er - de still ge - küßt, Daß sie im Blü - then - schim - mer Von
ceived from Heav'n a kiss, Her soul in rap - ture steep - ing And

ihm nur träu - men müßt. Die Luft ging durch die Fel - der, Die
bring - ing dreams of bliss. The stars were shi - ning bright - ly And

24

mei - ne See - le spann - te Weit ih - re Flü - gel aus, und
this my soul long pon - dered, At last her wings she spread, on

28

mei - ne See - le spann - te, und mei - ne See - le spann - te Weit
this my soul long pon - dered, on this my soul long pon - dered, At

32

ih - re Flü - gel aus, _____ Flog durch die stil - len
last her wings she spread, _____ And through the air _____ she

36

Lan - de, Als flö - ge sie nach Haus, _____ flog _ durch die stil - len,
wan - dered As though she home-ward sped, _____ and _ through the air _____

stil - len Lan - de,   als __ flö - ge sie __   nach ___ Haus.
she __ wan-dered   as __ though ___ she home - ward __ sped.

Spring

A Spring in the Desert I Found

George Parsons Lathrop

Foun - - - tain, Foun - tain of Lo - ver's Tears.

Clover Blossoms

Oscar Laighton

arms _____ of gold, O that these arms her form _____ might

fold, O that these arms _ her _ form _____ might fold!

Gen - tly the

breez - es kiss _____ her hair, She is so fair, ___ so _____

A Bird upon a Rosy Bough

Op. 40, No. 1

Celia Laighton Thaxter

waves that kiss a bar - ren shore, _____ In sob - bing

ca - dence, in sob-bing ca - dence died _____ the song. _____

A Farewell

Op. 40, No. 2

Charles Kingsley

Beneath the Starry Arch

Op. 40, No. 3

Harriet Martineau

Partsongs

Funeral Hymn for a Soldier

Op. 14, No. 1

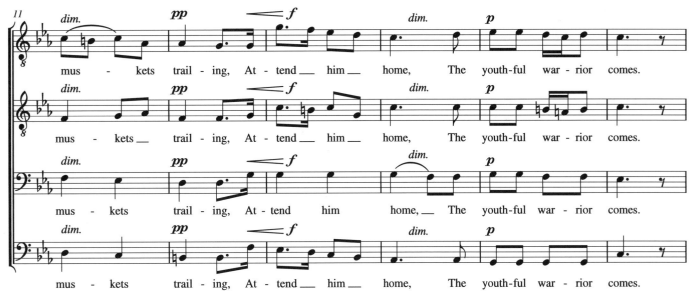

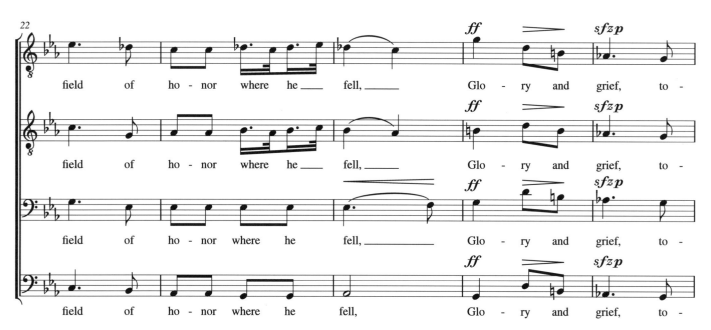

The Summer Webs

Op. 14, No. 2

Minstrel's Song

Op. 14, No. 3

Thomas Chatterton

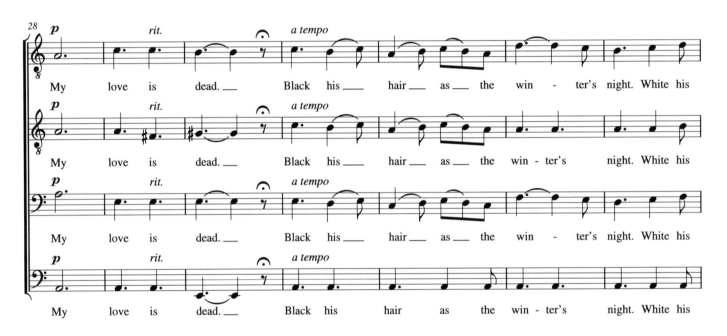

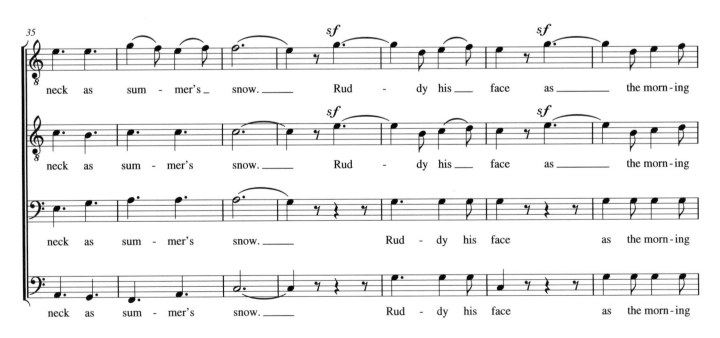

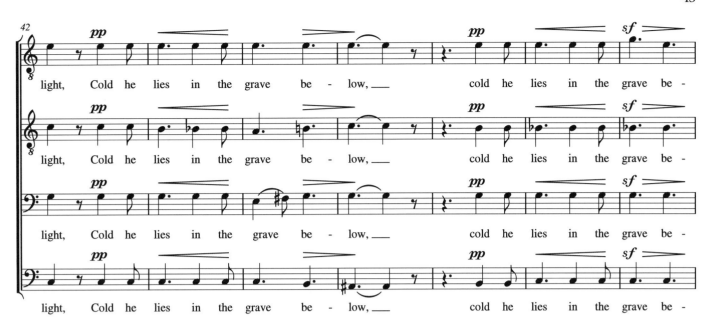

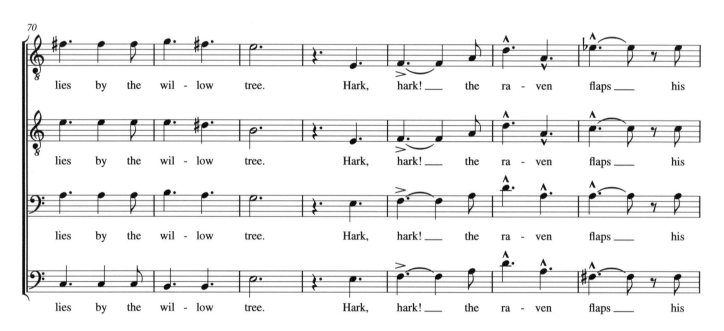

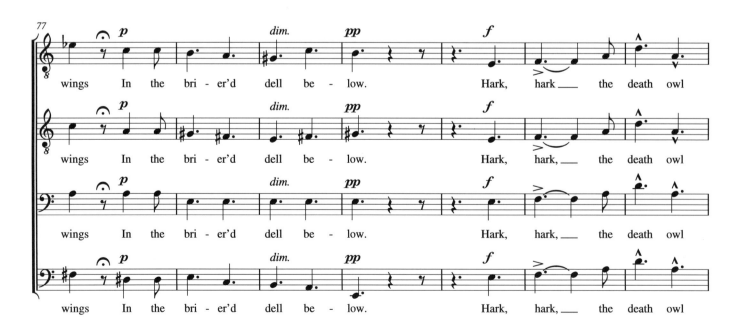

loud ____ doth sing To the night - mares as they ____ go. O

loud ____ doth sing To the night - mares as they go.

loud ____ doth sing To the night - mares as they go.

loud ____ doth sing To the night - mares as they go.

see the ____ white ____ moon ____ shines ____ on high; Whit - er is my true ____ love's

See the ____ white ____ moon ____ shines on high; Whit - er is my true love's

See the ____ white ____ moon ____ shines ____ on high; Whit - er is my true love's

See the white moon shines on high; Whit - er is my true love's

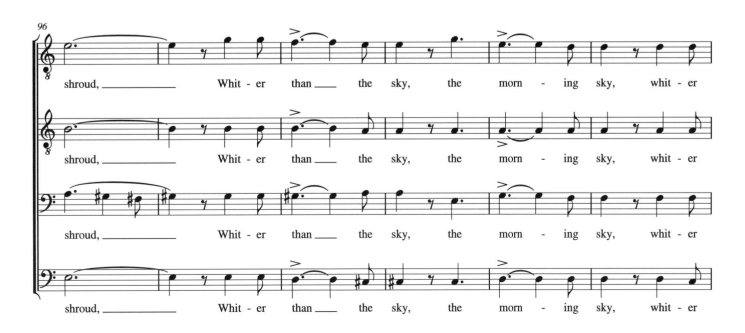

shroud, _____ Whit - er than ____ the sky, the morn - ing sky, whit - er

shroud, _____ Whit - er than ____ the sky, the morn - ing sky, whit - er

shroud, _____ Whit - er than ____ the sky, the morn - ing sky, whit - er

shroud, _____ Whit - er than ____ the sky, the morn - ing sky, whit - er

than ___ the eve - ning cloud. ___ My love ___ is dead, Gone

than the ___ eve - ning cloud. ___ My love ___ is dead, Gone

than the ___ eve - ning cloud. ___ My love ___ is dead, Gone

than the eve - ning cloud. ___ My love ___ is dead, Gone

to _____ his bed, All un - der the wil - low tree.

to _____ his bed, All un - der the wil - low tree.

to _____ his bed, All un - der the wil - low tree.

to _____ his bed, All un - der the wil - low tree.

Peace, Peace to Him That's Gone

Version 1

Thomas Moore

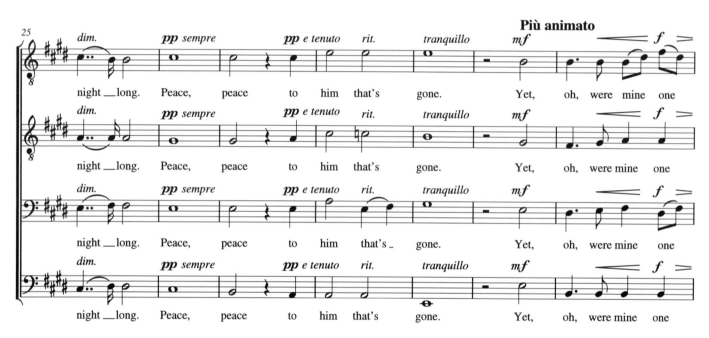

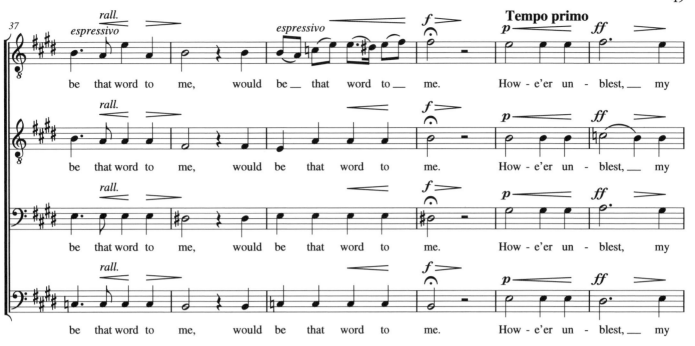

Peace, Peace to Him That's Gone

Version 2

Thomas Moore

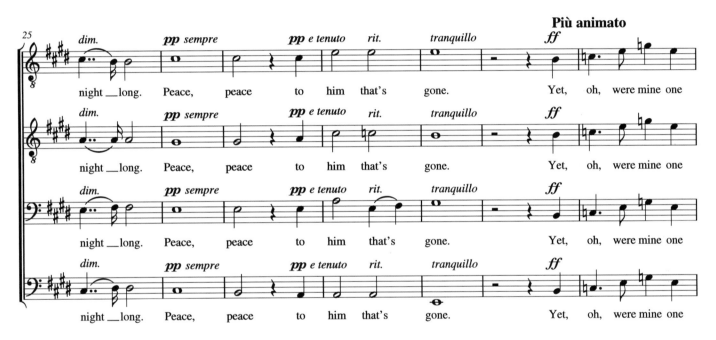

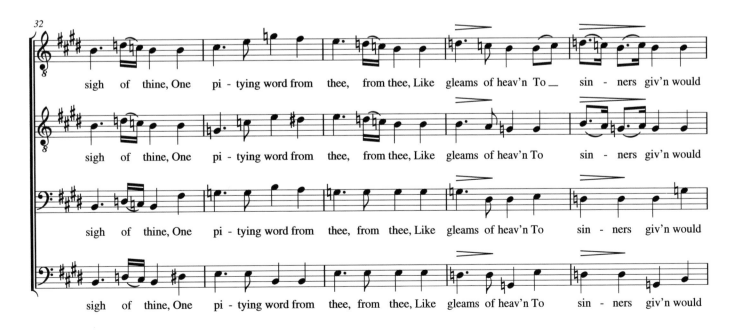

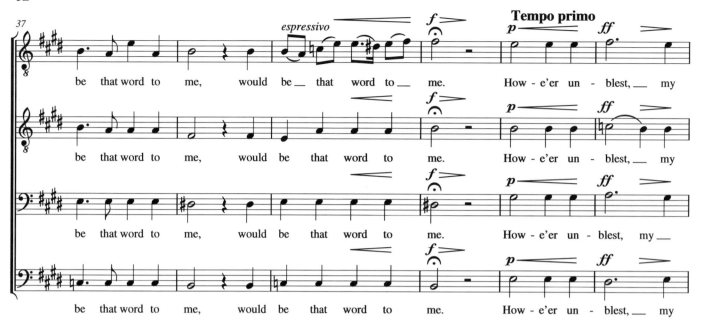

Radway's Ready Relief

Dr. Dolore

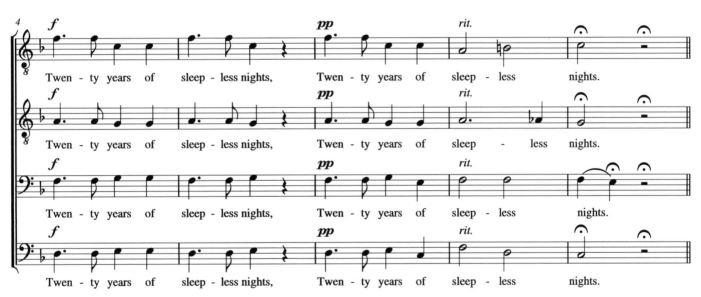

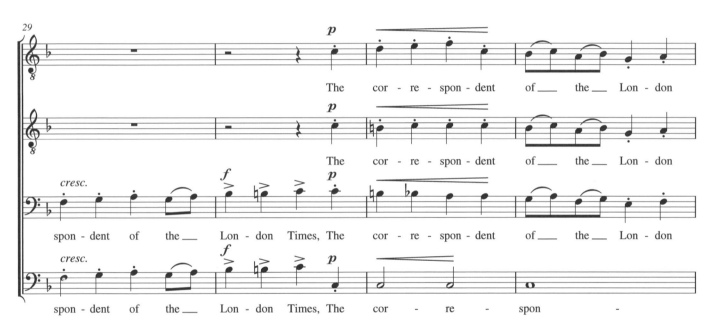

lief, Rad-way's Read-y Re-lief, Rad - way's Read - y Re - lief.

lief, Rad-way's Read-y Re-lief, Rad - way's Read y Re - lief.

lief, He ap - plied Rad-way's Read-y Re-lief, Rad - way's Read - y Re - lief.

lief, He ap - plied Rad-way's Read-y Re-lief, Rad - way's Read - y Re - lief.

SOLO *Recit. ad lib.*

It im - me - di-ate-ly gave him rest And se-cur'd him the first

Grave *(impressively)*

calm and un-dis-tur - - - bed sleep dur - ing the twen-ty years.

*To be whistled or played by Piccolo Flute.

Soldier's Oath

Charles Timothy Brooks

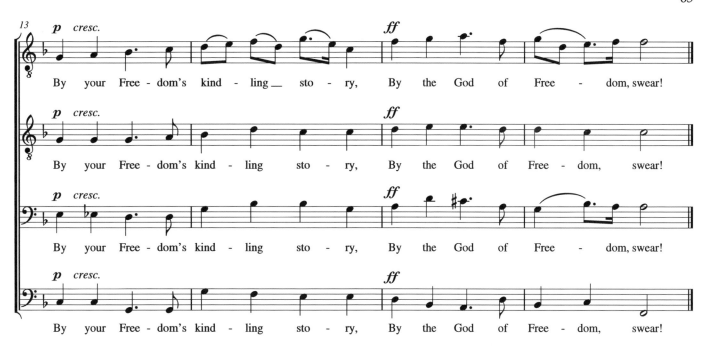

Lift on high both heart and hand!
Swear, that earth and heaven may hear it,
And the brazen traitor fear it,
Swear the oath to save your land!
Glorious ensign, float before us,
Proudly lead us to the field!
While thy folds are fluttering o'er us,
None shall basely flee or yield.

Lift on high both heart and hand!
Swell, with Freedom's pure air filling,
Noble flag! each bosom thrilling
Of our chosen patriot band.
Sign of honor! never paling,
Save in death, our cheeks thou'lt see,
Thousand pangs with transport hailing,
Ere we turn our backs on thee!

Lift on high both heart and hand!
Hail, this glorious consecration!
Hail, regenerated nation!
Hail, all hail! thou newborn land!
Sons of Freedom, all assemble,
Solemn vows and praise to pay!
Falsehood, fraud, and treason, tremble!
Courage, children of the day!

Lift on high both heart and hand!
To the King of Nations rear it,
Let the great Heart-Searcher hear it,
As we here before him stand,
Praying him to keep us holy,
Pure in thought and word and deed,
Him whose hand uplifts the lowly,
Makes the just alone succeed!

O Bless the Lord, My Soul

Isaac Watts

Critical Report

Library Sigla

DLC-Mu   Library of Congress, Music Division
MB   Boston Public Library
MH-Ar   Harvard University Archives
MH-H   Harvard University, Houghton Library
MH-W   Harvard University, Widener Library

Editorial Methods

The manuscripts are carefully and clearly copied and present few problems in transcription. In works with more than one source, the notation of the music as presented in the principal sources has been retained as much as possible, with material from earlier or secondary sources incorporated in cases of error or missing notation. All such changes are reported in the critical notes.

Editorial cautionary accidentals are placed in parentheses; all other editorial additions are enclosed in square brackets. Instances of nonstandard stem direction and beaming have been tacitly regularized, as has notation of rests according to modern convention. Vocal parts have been transcribed using beams for note values less than a quarter note. Certain slurring practices have been normalized, particularly the use of a single slur to connect two or more chords and the inclusion of tied notes within a slur both at the beginning and end of a slurred passage. Instances of a notehead being used for both undotted and dotted values (such as a dotted quarter note being combined with the first note of an eighth- or sixteenth-note grouping) have been renotated, as in the beginning of *A Bird upon a Rosy Bough*. The placement of phrasing, articulation marks (accents, staccato dots, tenuto dashes, etc.), groupette identifiers, and pedal indications have been normalized.

Nonstandard abbreviations (e.g., *cres.* for *cresc.*, *sosten.* for *sost.*, and *ritard.* for *rit.*) have been tacitly regularized. Most source cautionary accidentals (usually provided to "cancel" inflections in previous measures) have been retained, particularly those that would prevent possible misreadings especially in chromatic passages; source cautionaries deemed superfluous have been deleted with report.

Critical Notes

Critical notes report rejected readings of sources. For pitch notation, I use the system in which middle C is indicated as c'. Chords are indicated with a plus sign, with pitches listed from the bottom up.

Matin Song

Sources

A. MB, **M.451.209. Autograph manuscript.
B. "Matin Song," in *Atlantic Monthly* 39 (January 1877): 110–11.
C. "Matin Song," No. 1 from *Four Songs by John K. Paine* (Boston: Oliver Ditson & Co., 1879).
D. *Matin Song* (Boston: Oliver Ditson & Co., 1889). Lower key (F).
E. "Matin Song," in *Songs by Thirty Americans*, ed. Rupert Hughes (Ditson, 1904).
F. *Matin Song* (Boston: Oliver Ditson Co., 1907).

Notes

This edition is based on C.

M. 1 is a pasted in addition in A.   M. 2, Voice, *p* in D.   M. 8, Voice, decrescendo wedge in D.   M. 8, Pn., RH, slur lacking in A.   Mm. 9 and 29, Pn., note 2, RH d♮' is eighth in E.   M. 10, Pn., LH, slur lacking in A.   M. 15, Voice, beats 2 and 3, decrescendo wedge in D; Pn., decrescendo wedge lacking in A and B.   Mm. 18 and 38, Pn., RH, d♭ dotted quarter notated as quarter tied to eighth in E.   Mm. 20 and 40, Pn., RH, beat 3, tenuto lacking in B, D, and E; LH, slur from e♭ to g; RH lower voice and LH slurs lacking in B.   M. 20, Pn., LH, d♭ is dotted in A.   M. 26, Voice, note 2, eighth in C.   M. 27, Voice, crescendo wedge lacking in A.   M. 30, Pn., LH, slur lacking in A.   M. 35, Pn., decrescendo wedge lacking in A and B, appears instead in m. 36 in place of *dim*.   M. 36, Voice, period instead of exclamation point in D; *dim*. lacking in C and D, notated as decrescendo wedge in A and B.   M. 39, Voice, exclamation point in B.

I Wore your Roses Yesterday

Sources

A. "I Wore your Roses Yesterday," No. 2 from *Four Songs by John K. Paine* (Boston: Oliver Ditson & Co., 1879).
B. Poem published as "Song" in *Atlantic Monthly* 36 (August 1875): 151.

Notes

M. 37, Pn., beat 2; ritard.   M. 45, Pn., beat 2, a tempo. M. 47, Voice, beat 1, b♭'–a♭'–g' notated as dotted sixteenth–thirty-second–sixteenth.

Early Spring-time

SOURCES

A. MH-H, fMS Mus 57.44 (2). Autograph manuscript.
B. "Early Spring-time," No. 3 from *Four Songs by John K. Paine* (Boston: Oliver Ditson & Co., 1879).

NOTES

A is dated, "Cambridge, June 28, 1866." A number of revisions were made for the 1879 publication, including the repetition of "the longing" in mm. 8–9, rebarring the following measure in ¾, and adding the final two measures for the piano. Many changes in piano figurations, note values, and articulations were incorporated into the published edition. A German text, written above the vocal staff in the autograph, was omitted in the 1879 edition. This edition is based on B, with the German text added from A.

Three tempo indications in A: *With feeling, and moderately slow; Gefühlvoll, in mäßiger Bewegung;* and *Andante moderato, con anima.* M. 1 (pickup), Pn., *delicato* in A; RH, tenuto and accent lacking in A. M. 2, Pn., tenutos, decrescendo wedge lacking in A. M. 3, Pn., *dim.* lacking in A. M. 4, Pn., LH fermata and *rall.* lacking in A; *pp* on beat 2 in A. M. 5, Voice, *With feeling* lacking in A; Pn., *m.v.* and *legato* in A. Mm. 5 to 7, beat 1, Pn., slurs lacking in A. M. 7, Voice, beat 2, eighth rest, eighth d♯″, slurred to following measure, in A; text is first syllable of "mingled"; Pn., beat 2, eighth rest, eighth-note chord (RH a′+d♯″; LH f♯+b♯) in A. M. 8 lacking in A. M. 9, Voice, beat 1, sixteenths e″, e″, eighth c♯″, first note in slur from previous measure, in A; text is "mingled with"; Pn., beat 1, eighth-note chords (RH g♯′+e″, e′+c♯″; LH g♯+c♯′, a+c♯′), in slur from last chord of previous measure, in A. M. 10 notated as m. 9, beat 2, plus m. 10 in A; no change of meter. M. 10 (renotated), Voice, f♯′ quarter note, eighth rest, g♯′ eighth, slurred to first of sixteenths a′, a′, eighth c♯″, in A; crescendo wedge from A; Pn., RH, beat 2 (separate eighth chord) staccato, remaining eighths in slur, f♯′ quarter notated as two eighths, in A; LH, beat 1 in slur, beat 2 staccato, remaining eighths are dyads (g♯+b, f♯+a, e+a), in A. M. 11, Pn., decrescendo wedge lacking in A. Mm. 12 and 13, Pn., beat 1, eighths slurred in two-note groups with second note staccato in A; LH middle voice is octave doubling of bass notes in A. M. 13, Pn., beat 2, RH, no grace note in A, LH, dyad, f♯′+c♯″, tied to following measure, in A; *sf* on beat 2 in A. M. 14, Voice, d♯″ eighth, two eighth rests, d♯″ eighth in A; Pn., beat 2, eighth-note chord (RH a′+d♯″; LH f♯+b♯), in A. M. 15, Pn., beat 1, RH, eighths e″, c♯″ over quarter g♯′, beat 2 eighth dyads f♯′+a′, e′+g♯′; LH, quarter dyad e+c♯′, eighth dyads f♯+c♯′, g♯+b, in A. M. 16, *rit. poco,* in A; Pn., beat 1, chord includes e′ in A. Mm. 16 and 17, Pn., beat 1, slurs lacking in A. M. 17, Pn., *a tempo* on first beat, *p* and *delicato* on last eighth, in A; *a tempo* lacking in voice in A. M. 18, Pn., beat 1, dotted quarter g♯′ notated as quarter, eighth in A. M. 20, Pn., *m.v.* in A. M. 20 to m. 22, beat one, Pn., slurs lacking in A. M. 22, Pn., beat two, last chord, RH f♯′+d♯″, LH f♯+b, in A.

M. 23, Voice, beat one, two sixteenths and eighth; Pn., RH dyads e′+e″, e′+c♯″, LH dyads g♯+b, a+c♯′, dyads are slurred in A; Pn., crescendo wedge in A. M. 24, Pn., beat 2, RH, dyads d♯″+g♯″, e″+g♯″, in A. M. 25, Pn., beat 1, *sf;* RH dyad b♯′+g♯″ in A; beat 2, Voice and Pn., *p* in A. M. 26, Voice and Pn., beat 2, RH, double-dotted eighth, thirty-second, e″, d♯″, in A. Mm. 28–29 written as single measure in A: Voice, quarter, two eighths; Pn., quarter-note chords; wedges lacking in A, *p* in A, *solemnly* and *solenne* in voice part in A. M. 31, Voice, beat 2, eighth rest, sixteenths c♯″, c♯″, in A; Pn., eighth chords slurred in twos, with second eighth staccato in A; grace note lacking in A. M. 33, Pn., ties from previous measure lacking in A; LH, beat 2, dyad, A+a in A; Voice, beat 2, *Rit. e piano* in A. M. 34, Pn., beat one, RH, a′ lacking from chord, LH, dyad B+a (upper note tied to previous measure), in A; *p* on beat 2 in A. M. 35, Pn., last chord lacking, along with mm. 36–37, in A.

Mondnacht (Moonlight)

SOURCES

A. MH-H, fMS Mus 57.44 (6). Autograph manuscript.
B. "Moonlight. Mondnacht," No. 4 from *Four Songs by John K. Paine* (Boston: Oliver Ditson & Co., 1879).

NOTES

English title lacking in A. Dated "1867" in A. This edition is based on B.

M. 7, Pn., RH, beat 2, f♯″, f♯′ in B. M. 13, Voice, beats 2 and 3 dotted quarter, sixteenth rest, sixteenth, in A. Mm. 14–16, Pn., pedal markings lacking in A. Mm. 15–20, Pn., RH slur lacking in A. Mm. 18–19, Pn., *poco marcato* lacking in A. M. 19, Pn., beats 2 and 3, LH accents in A. M. 29, Pn., beats 1 and 2, RH, eighths are c♯″, c♯″ in B. M. 44, Pn., beat 3, slur lacking in B.

Spring

SOURCE

MH-H, fMS Mus 57.42. Autograph manuscript.

NOTES

Source dated at end: "Aug. 9, 1869, Constableville, N.Y."

M. 2, Voice, notes 2–3, eighths. M. 7, Voice, note 3 has cautionary natural. M. 20, Voice, notes 2–3, eighths. M. 24, Voice, note 3, d♭″. M. 25, Pn., LH, dyads 2–4 written as upper notes with octave signs. M. 26, meter signature added to regularize incomplete measure.

A Spring in the Desert I Found

SOURCE

DLC-Mu, ML96.P2. Autograph manuscript.

NOTES

Autograph headings: "Song: 'A spring in the desert I found.' / Words by G. P. Lathrop, composed by J. K. Paine." Added in a later hand, not Paine's: "Composed about 1878"; in another hand: "The Fountain."

M. 15, Voice, notes 2–3, g#′, b′.   M. 33, Pn., notes 5–6, RH, d#′, c#″; note 8, c#″.   M. 53, text, "Lover's" not capitalized.

Clover Blossoms

SOURCE

A. MH-H, fMS Mus 57.44 (1). Autograph manuscript.
B. "Clover Blossoms" in Oscar Laighton, *Ninety years at the Isles of Shoals* (Boston: Beacon Press, 1930), 76.

NOTES

Title page: " 'The clover blossoms kiss her feet.' / Song by / Oscar Laighton: / composed by / John K. Paine." Dated at end: "Cambridge, Oct. 1, 1882."
M. 12, Voice, rhythm quarter, eighth rest, eighth.   M. 18, Pn., notes 4–5, RH, b′, g′.   M. 40, Voice, rhythm quarter, eighth rest, eighth.   M. 46, Pn., notes 4–5, RH, b′–g′.   M. 66, Voice, rhythm quarter, eighth rest, eighth.   M. 72, Pn., notes 4–5, RH, b′–g′.

A Bird upon a Rosy Bough

SOURCES

A. "A bird upon a rosy bough," No. 1 from *Four Songs by John Knowles Paine, Op. 40* (Boston: Arthur P. Schmidt & Co., 1884).
B. Poem published in *The Poems of Celia Thaxter* (Boston: Houghton, Mifflin, and Co., 1896), 229.

NOTES

Mm. 12 and 14, 22 and 24, 31 and 33, text, comma instead of dash in A.   Mm. 15–16, text, "Love" and "Death" not capitalized in A; comma after "Death" in A. Mm. 30–31, text, quotation marks lacking in A.

A Farewell

SOURCES

A. "A farewell," No. 2 from *Four Songs by John Knowles Paine, Op. 40* (Boston: Arthur P. Schmidt & Co., 1885).
B. Poem published in *Charles Kingsley: His Letters and Memories of his Life* (London: Macmillan & Co., Ltd., 1901) II, 236; and Charles Kingsley, *Poems* (London: Macmillan & Co., Ltd., 1902), 281.

NOTES

Middle verse is lacking in A, and is taken from B.
M. 10, Voice, verse 3, "and" is lacking in A.

Beneath the Starry Arch

SOURCES

A. "Beneath the starry arch," No. 3 from *Four Songs by John Knowles Paine, Op. 40* (Boston: Arthur P. Schmidt & Co., 1885).
B. The first thirteen measures are reproduced in Louis C. Elson, *The History of American Music* (1904; rev. 1915).

NOTES

M. 27, Pn., LH, B♭ half.   M. 42, Pn., LH, E♭ half.

Funeral Hymn for a Soldier

SOURCE

MH-H, fMS Mus 57.42. Autograph manuscript.

NOTES

Penciled notation, upper left corner of manuscript: "Transpose to D minor."

The Summer Webs

SOURCE

MH-H, fMS Mus 57.44 (11). Autograph manuscript.

NOTE

Title: "Part Song."

Minstrel's Song

SOURCE

DLC-Mu, ML96.P2. Autograph manuscript.

NOTE

Notation, upper left corner: "Composed about 1863."

Peace, Peace to Him That's Gone (both versions)

SOURCE

MH-H, fMS Mus 57.44 (7). Autograph manuscript.

NOTES

Title: "Part Song: 'Peace, peace to him that's gone.' " Notations, upper left corner: "No. 2"; "For Male voices"; "Transpose to F."
M. 15, B, redundant *cresc.*   Mm. 37 and 39, *espressivo*.

Radway's Ready Relief

SOURCES

A. MB, [John K. Paine], *Radway's Ready Relief,* Property of the Apollo Club of Boston. Composed By Dr Dolore, 1883.
B. John K. Paine, *Radway's Ready Relief,* As sung by the Apollo Club, of Boston. Male Quartet, with Bass Solo (Composed in 1863) (Boston: Oliver Ditson & Co.).

NOTES

Both sources have "Copyright, 1883 by Davenport Bros." at the bottom of the first page of music. The edition is based on A.
M. 8, *ritard.* in B.   M. 24, *accel. poco a poco* lacking in B. M. 40, all, redundant *dim.*   M. 43, *Adagio e doloroso* in B. M. 49, all, redundant *cresc.*   M. 134, footnote, "To be whistled" in A; reading of edition from B.

Soldier's Oath

SOURCE

MH-Ar, Program booklet, *Harvard College, Commemoration Day, July 21, 1865;* copy bound into Sibley's Private Journal.

O Bless the Lord, My Soul

SOURCE

John Knowles Paine, *O bless the Lord, my soul,* Anthem for Men's Voices, Revised and edited by Charles Leslie (Boston: G. Schirmer, 1911).